Sports Illustrated KIDS

SIDE BY SIDE

BASEBALL STARS

Comparing Pro Baseball's Greatest Players

BY MATT CHANDLER

CAPSTONE PRESS
a capstone imprint

SIDE-BY-SIDE BASEBALL STARS:
Comparing Pro Baseball's Greatest Players

Baseball is a game built on match-ups. Fans loved to watch Pedro Martinez stare down Derek Jeter with the game on the line. Would Martinez blow a 95-mph fastball by the Yankees captain? Or would Jeter anticipate the pitch and drive the ball into the seats for a game-winning home run? The two superstars faced each other 107 times in the regular season. Jeter notched 29 hits off of Martinez, which is the same number of times Martinez struck out the Yankee captain.

Teams battle to win the World Series, and players square off with each at-bat. But what if the greatest players in the history of the game could go head-to-head? Imagine Hammerin' Hank trading home runs with the Babe. How about Reggie Jackson squaring off against Big Papi in October? Decide for yourself who comes out on top in some of baseball's toughest matchups.

*All stats are through the 2013 season.

Sports Illustrated Kids Side-By-Side Sports are published by Capstone Press, 1710 Roe Crest Drive, North Mankato, Minnesota 56003
www.capstonepub.com

Sports Illustrated Kids is a trademark of Time Inc. Used with permission.

Printed in the United States of America in Stevens Point, Wisconsin.
032014   008092WZF14

TABLE OF CONTENTS

DAVID ORTIZ VS. REGGIE JACKSON 4

HANK AARON VS. BABE RUTH 8

RICKEY HENDERSON VS. TY COBB 12

TED WILLIAMS VS. MIGUEL CABRERA 16

DEREK JETER VS. OZZIE SMITH 20

KEN GRIFFEY JR. VS. WILLIE MAYS 24

JOHNNY BENCH VS. YADIER MOLINA 28

CLAYTON KERSHAW VS. NOLAN RYAN 32

RANDY JOHNSON VS. SANDY KOUFAX
VS. TOM GLAVINE VS. TIM WAKEFIELD 36

MARIANO RIVERA VS. DENNIS ECKERSLEY 40

Manager's Call 44

Critical Thinking Using the Common Core 46

Quotation Sources 46

Read More 47

Internet Sites 47

Index 48

DAVID
ORTIZ

NICKNAME: Big Papi
HEIGHT: 6 feet, 4 inches (193 cm)
WEIGHT: 250 lbs (113 kg)
YEARS ACTIVE: 1997–present*
TEAMS: Twins, Red Sox
ALL-STAR GAMES: 9
WORLD SERIES RINGS: 3

Games	HRs	RBIs	Playoff Games	Playoff HRs	Playoff RBIs
1,969	431	1,429	82	17	60

*Stats are through the 2013 season.

REGGIE JACKSON

NICKNAME: Mr. October
HEIGHT: 6 feet (183 cm)
WEIGHT: 195 lbs (88 kg)
YEARS ACTIVE: 1967–1987
TEAMS: Athletics, Orioles, Yankees, Angels
ALL-STAR GAMES: 14
MVP AWARDS: 1
WORLD SERIES RINGS: 5
-*Entered the Hall of Fame in 1993*

Games	HRs	RBIs	Playoff Games	Playoff HRs	Playoff RBIs
2820	563	1702	77	18	48

DAVID ORTIZ

"I swing hard all the time. That's what I've done my whole life—hit." —*David Ortiz*

"I don't think you could ever ask for more out of an individual than what he does on and off the field." —*Teammate Jon Lester*

With more than 34,000 screaming fans on their feet, David Ortiz stepped to the plate for his first ever World Series at bat. It was October 23, 2004, and the Red Sox were playing in their first World Series in nearly 20 years. The team hadn't captured a championship since 1918, and Boston was counting on its slugger to end the drought. Big Papi took a mighty swing and drove the ball into the right field seats for a three-run home run. Ortiz hit 41 home runs during the regular season, but none were as clutch as his blast in Game 1. The Red Sox went on to sweep the St. Louis Cardinals.

Big Papi thrives in the spotlight. On the biggest stage, Ortiz always seems to deliver. In the 2013 World Series, he hit an incredible .688 and led the Red Sox to their third title in a decade.

REGGIE JACKSON

Of the many Hall of Fame players to wear Yankee pinstripes, few were as clutch at the plate as Reggie Jackson. He earned his nickname, "Mr. October," for his amazing play in the postseason. He smashed 18 playoff home runs in his career, including 10 in World Series play. Jackson was only a .267 career hitter, but with the game on the line, he always seemed to deliver. In 27 World Series games, Jackson hit .357.

The Yankees legend will always be remembered for his heroic hitting in Game 4 of the 1977 World Series. Jackson became the only player in World Series history to hit home runs in three consecutive at bats. The Yankees beat the Los Angeles Dodgers 8-4 and captured the club's 21st championship.

"The only reason I don't like playing in the World Series is I can't watch myself play."
—*Reggie Jackson*

"He's one of my favorite people in the world. He's an icon."
—*Former pitcher Dave Stewart*

HANK
AARON

NICKNAME: Hammerin' Hank
HEIGHT: 6 feet (183 cm)
WEIGHT: 180 lbs (81.6 kg)
YEARS ACTIVE: 1954–1976
TEAMS: Braves, Brewers
ALL-STAR GAMES: 25
MVP AWARDS: 1
BATTING TITLES: 2
GOLD GLOVES: 3
WORLD SERIES RINGS: 1
-Entered the Hall of Fame in 1982

Games	BA	HRs	RBIs	Runs
3,298	.305	755	2,297	2,174

BABE RUTH

NICKNAME: The Sultan of Swat
HEIGHT: 6 feet, 2 inches (188 cm)
WEIGHT: 215 lbs (97.5 kg)
YEARS ACTIVE: 1914–1935
TEAMS: Red Sox, Yankees, Braves
ALL-STAR GAMES: 2 (The first All-Star Game
    was in 1933; Ruth's last season was 1935)
MVP AWARDS: 1
BATTING TITLES: 1
WORLD SERIES RINGS: 7
-Entered the Hall of Fame in 1936

Games	BA	HRs	RBIs	Runs
2,503	.342	714	2,220	2,174

Barry Bonds holds the official record for most home runs in the history of Major League Baseball, smacking 762 over a 22-year career. But many fans will tell you Hank Aaron is the true home run king. "Hammerin' Hank" hit 755 home runs while playing for the Braves in Milwaukee and Atlanta.

Part of what made Aaron great was his consistency and durability. He played in 3,298 major league games—third on the all-time list. His power was consistent too. He had 15 seasons with 30 or more home runs. In eight of those seasons, he had at least 40 long balls. His consistency helped him climb the list of career home run hitters. Aaron reached his career total of 755 homers without ever hitting 50 in a single season.

"Guessing what the pitcher is going to throw is 80% of being a successful hitter."

—Hank Aaron

"He was awesome. He could do everything."

—Joe Torre, former manager and former teammate of Aaron

BABE RUTH

When you think of George Herman "Babe" Ruth, you probably imagine towering home runs. The Babe was known for his power, hitting 714 home runs during his Hall of Fame career. At the start of the 1920 season, no player had ever hit 30 home runs in a season. Ruth smacked 54 long balls that year. He followed that with 59 home runs the next season. In 1927 he became the first player to hit 60 home runs in a season. Those numbers made Ruth the first real power hitter in the game.

Did you know that Ruth was also a dominant pitcher? He was considered one of the best hurlers of his era, once tossing $29\frac{2}{3}$ scoreless innings in World Series play. In the 1916 and 1918 World Series, Ruth was a combined 3-0 with a 0.87 ERA on the hill. He stopped pitching in 1921 to focus on hitting, but he made two starts late in his career, winning both games. Although he was an impressive pitcher, it was Ruth's knack for hitting the long ball that made him a crowd favorite in Boston and New York.

"Baseball was, is, and always will be to me the best game in the world."
—*Babe Ruth*

"No one hit home runs the way Babe did. They were something special." —*Teammate Lefty Gomez*

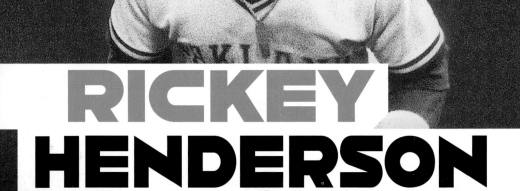

RICKEY
HENDERSON

NICKNAME: Man of Steal

HEIGHT: 5 feet, 10 inches (178 cm)

WEIGHT: 180 lbs (82 kg)

YEARS ACTIVE: 1979–2003

TEAMS: Athletics, Yankees, Blue Jays, Padres, Angels, Mets, Mariners, Red Sox, Dodgers

ALL-STAR GAMES: 10

MVP AWARDS: 1

WORLD SERIES RINGS: 2

-Led league in stolen bases 12 times

-Entered the Hall of Fame in 2009

Games	BA	Hits	Runs	Stolen Bases
3,081	.279	3,055	2,295	1,406

TY
COBB

NICKNAME: The Georgia Peach
HEIGHT: 6 feet, 1 inch (185 cm)
WEIGHT: 175 lbs (79 kg)
YEARS ACTIVE: 1905–1928
TEAMS: Tigers, Athletics
ALL-STAR GAMES: Played before the
   All-Star Game existed
MVP AWARDS: 1
BATTING TITLES: 12

-Led league in stolen bases six times
-Led league in runs five times
-Entered the Hall of Fame in 1936

Games	BA	Hits	Runs	Stolen Bases
3,034	.366	4,189	2,246	897

RICKEY HENDERSON

With more than a month left in the 1982 season, the Oakland Athletics' Rickey Henderson was tied with Lou Brock for the single-season stolen base record with 118. During a late August game against the Milwaukee Brewers, Henderson took a lead off of first base. After four pickoff attempts by the pitcher, Henderson stole second, barely beating the tag. He was the new single-season record holder. He ended the season with 130 steals—a record that has held for more than 30 years.

Henderson was one of the fastest men to play the game. He stole 1,406 bases in the regular season, plus another 33 in the postseason. Henderson was a threat to score with every hit, and his speed alone could change the outcome of a game. He was also a master at distracting opposing pitchers as he danced around while leading off from a base.

"Rickey Henderson is the number one disruptive force in the American League."

—*Former Yankees pitcher Dave Righetti*

"If my uniform doesn't get dirty, I haven't done anything in the baseball game." —*Rickey Henderson*

TY COBB

"Baseball was 100% of my life."
—*Ty Cobb*

"The burning desire to excel. That was Ty Cobb, the greatest ball player who ever lived."
—*Hall of Famer Frank "Home Run" Baker*

Pitchers couldn't keep Ty Cobb off base, and he made them pay for it. The Georgia Peach reached base an incredible 5,532 times in his career. Cobb is one of only two men in the history of the game to collect more than 4,000 hits. He stretched hundreds of those hits into extra bases with his speed.

Many of Cobb's 892 career stolen bases came as a result of his aggressive style of base running. He was known to slide hard into second base with his spikes high. If the fielder held his ground, he risked getting injured. That fear gave Cobb an edge on the base paths, and he used it to his advantage. Many players thought Cobb was a dirty player, and there were even rumors that he sharpened his spikes to intentionally injure his opponents. Despite his style of play, few can argue that Cobb was one of the biggest threats on the base paths that baseball has ever seen.

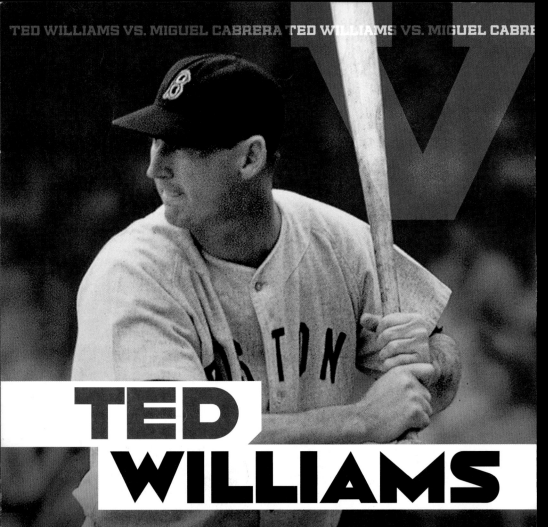

TED
WILLIAMS

NICKNAME: : The Splendid Splinter
HEIGHT: 6 feet, 3 inches (190 cm)
WEIGHT: 205 lbs (93 kg)
YEARS ACTIVE: 1939–1942, 1946–1960
TEAM: Red Sox
ALL-STAR GAMES: 19
MVP AWARDS: 2
BATTING TITLES: 6
-*Entered the Hall of Fame in 1966*

Games	BA	Hits	HRs	RBIs	Runs
2,292	.344	2,654	521	1,839	1,798

MIGUEL
CABRERA

NICKNAME: Miggy
HEIGHT: 6 feet, 4 inches (193 cm)
WEIGHT: 240 lbs (109 kg)
YEARS ACTIVE: 2003–present*
TEAMS: Marlins, Tigers
ALL-STAR GAMES: 8
MVP AWARDS: 2
BATTING TITLES: 3
WORLD SERIES RINGS: 1

Games	BA	Hits	HRs	RBIs	Runs
1,660	.321	1,995	365	1,260	1,064

*Stats are through the 2013 season.

Hitting a game-winning home run to end your career is a dream for any player. For Red Sox legend Ted Williams, it was a dream that came true. On September 28, 1960, Williams stepped to the plate for the last time. He jumped on a 1-1 fastball and launched it into the right field bullpen. He later called the game-winning home run "a storybook finish."

After just four seasons in the big leagues, Williams missed three seasons while serving his country in World War II. But he returned right where he left off and continued his amazing career. Williams was a lifetime .344 hitter and is the last player to hit over .400 in a single season, batting .406 in 1941. Pure hitters like Williams are patient and don't swing at bad pitches very often. He led the league in walks eight times. His careful hitting eye helped make him one of the most dominant hitters in baseball.

"He was absolutely the best hitter I ever saw."
—*Hall of Famer Joe DiMaggio on Williams*

"He studied hitting the way a broker studies the stock market."
—*Former Red Sox outfielder Carl Yastrzemski*

Detroit Tigers infielder Miguel Cabrera has shown the ability to hit for both power and a high average during his career. He hit 30 or more home runs in nine of his first 11 seasons. He also topped a .320 batting average eight times. Pitchers beware: Miggy hasn't shown any signs of slowing down at the plate.

In 2012 Cabrera put it all together in one remarkable offensive season. His .330 batting average, 44 home runs, and 139 RBIs earned him the Triple Crown. Cabrera was the first player to lead his league in all three categories since Carl Yastrzemski did it in 1967. Cabrera accomplished the amazing feat at age 29, and Tigers fans are eager to see if he can repeat the crown.

"He's the best hitter in the game."
—*Los Angeles Angels outfielder Mike Trout*

"I'm just trying to play my best and have fun." —*Miguel Cabrera, late in the 2012 season as he closed in on the Triple Crown*

DEREK
JETER

NICKNAME: Captain Clutch
HEIGHT: 6 feet, 3 inches (190 cm)
WEIGHT: 195 lbs (88 kg)
YEARS ACTIVE: 1995–present*
TEAM: Yankees
GOLD GLOVES: 5
ALL-STAR GAMES: 13
WORLD SERIES RINGS: 5
-Led AL in fielding percentage twice

Games	Fielding %	Putouts	Assists	Errors
2,602	.976	3,676	6,349	243

*Stats are through the 2013 season.

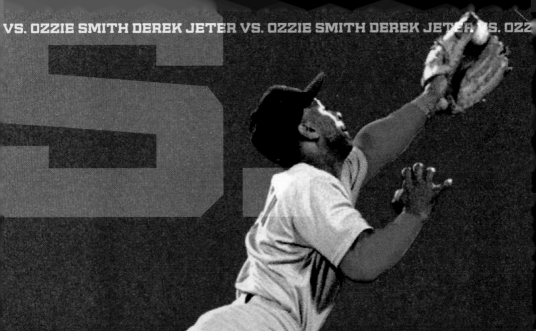

OZZIE SMITH

NICKNAME: The Wizard of Oz
HEIGHT: 5 feet, 11 inches (180 cm)
WEIGHT: 150 lbs (68 kg)
YEARS ACTIVE: 1978–1996
TEAMS: Padres, Cardinals
GOLD GLOVES: 13
ALL-STAR GAMES: 15
WORLD SERIES RINGS: 1

-Entered the Hall of Fame in 2002
-Led NL in fielding percentage eight times

Games	Fielding %	Putouts	Assists	Errors
2,573	.978	4,249	8,375	281

DEREK JETER

"He's unbelievable. If he's not the full package, I haven't seen one."

—*Former Yankees manager Stump Merrill*

"In big games, the action slows down for him where it speeds up for others."

—*Reggie Jackson*

On a humid July night in the Bronx, the New York Yankees were locked in a battle with the rival Boston Red Sox. The game was tied 3-3 in the 12th inning and the Red Sox had runners on second and third. With two outs, Trot Nixon looped a popup toward the seats. Yankees shortstop Derek Jeter raced toward the ball at full speed. With his glove outstretched, he made what many call the greatest catch of his career. His momentum carried him headfirst into the stands. He climbed back to the field—bloody and bruised—but still clutching the ball in his glove. The Yankees went on to win the game, though Jeter wasn't there to celebrate. He was at the hospital.

Jeter hit the big leagues with a bang in 1996 and earned the AL Rookie of the Year award. In nearly two decades as the Yankees shortstop, he has found a way to make the big plays. He is considered to be a lock for the Hall of Fame once he retires, which he announced would be after the 2014 season.

Every time Ozzie Smith stepped onto the field, fans expected something magical to happen. Smith used to start each game by jogging out to his shortstop position and doing a cartwheel into a backflip. It was his personal warm-up routine and part of the reason fans loved to watch him play.

Ozzie was known for his range—his ability to get to a ball anywhere near his position. He stole hits from his opponents with his glove, which made him a pitcher's best friend. During his 19-year career, The Wizard of Oz recorded 4,249 putouts at shortstop, which put him eighth on the all-time list.

"I didn't hit for a high average and I didn't hit home runs. I think I still did the things that don't necessarily show up in statistics."
—Ozzie Smith

"I don't think anybody ever played the position any better than he played it."
—Former Cardinals manager Whitey Herzog

KEN
GRIFFEY JR.

NICKNAME: Junior
HEIGHT: 6 feet, 3 inches (190 cm)
WEIGHT: 195 lbs (88 kg)
YEARS ACTIVE: 1989–2010
TEAMS: Mariners, Reds, White Sox
GOLD GLOVES: 10
ALL-STAR GAMES: 13
MVP AWARDS: 1
-Ranks sixth on the all-time HR list

Games	Fielding %	Putouts	Assists	Errors
2,671	.985	5,605	154	89

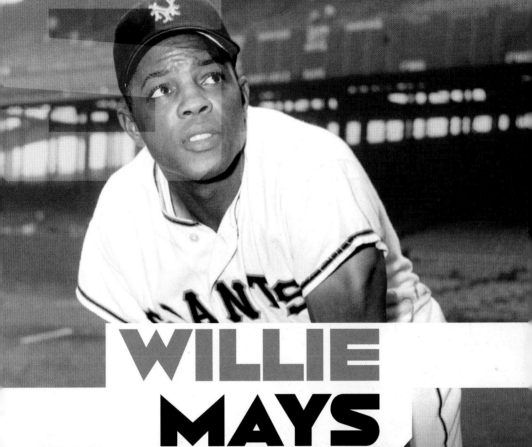

WILLIE
MAYS

NICKNAME: The "Say Hey" Kid
HEIGHT: 5 feet, 10 inches (178 cm)
WEIGHT: 170 lbs (77 kg)
YEARS ACTIVE: 1951–1952, 1954–1973
TEAMS: Giants, Mets
GOLD GLOVES: 12
ALL-STAR GAMES: 24
MVP AWARDS: 2
WORLD SERIES RINGS: 1
-Ranks fourth on the all-time HR list
-Entered the Hall of Fame in 1979

Games	Fielding %	Putouts	Assists	Errors
2,992	.981	7,095	195	89

KEN GRIFFEY JR.

Fans pay top dollar for seats behind a dugout in every major league stadium. But when outfielder Ken Griffey Jr. was playing, fans fought for the center field bleacher seats. It was there that they had the best view of Griffey streaking across the field and taking away extra bases from hitters. The lucky ones would get to see Griffey climb the outfield walls like Spiderman and rob home runs. He was so well-known for his defense that he was featured in the movie *Little Big League* making a game-ending catch over the fence.

Griffey could change the momentum of any game with his glove. Perhaps his most impressive catch was on April 26, 1990, in Yankee Stadium. It looked as if Yankees' outfielder Jesse Barfield had launched his 200th career home run over the wall in left centerfield. But Griffey raced into the gap, timed his leap perfectly, and snatched Barfield's would-be milestone.

"Guys like him don't come around every day. He's just as magical off the field as on it."

—*Former Mariners teammate Milton Bradley*

"Junior is the ultimate gamer. He plays the game hard. He plays the game right. He plays the game hurt." —*Former Reds Manager Bob Boone*

WILLIE MAYS

In Game One of the 1954 World Series, centerfielder Willie Mays and the underdog New York Giants were playing the Cleveland Indians. In the eighth inning, Cleveland's Vic Wertz crushed a ball to deep center field. Mays turned and sprinted, his back to home plate. Running directly toward the centerfield wall, he stuck out his glove and made what came to be called "The Catch." He robbed Wertz of at least a triple and set the tone of the World Series. Mays' Giants went on to win Game One and sweep the Indians in four games.

Great players rise up in the biggest moments, and Mays was among the greatest to ever play the game. In a big league career that lasted 22 years, he collected 12 Gold Gloves for his defense. He also holds the major league record for consecutive All-Star Games played with 24 (there were two All-Star Games played each season between 1959 and 1962).

"Outside of Joe DiMaggio, Willie Mays is the greatest all-around baseball player of my time."

—*Yankee legend Mickey Mantle*

"They invented the All-Star Game for Willie Mays."

—*Red Sox legend Ted Williams*

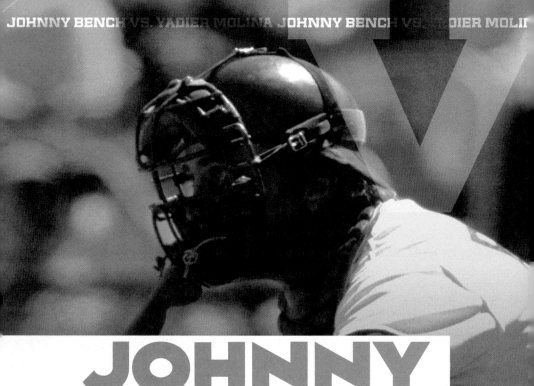

JOHNNY BENCH

NICKNAME: Little General
HEIGHT: 6 feet, 1 inch (185 cm)
WEIGHT: 197 lbs (89 kg)
YEARS ACTIVE: 1967–1983
TEAM: Reds
GOLD GLOVES: 10
ALL-STAR GAMES: 14
MVP AWARDS: 2
WORLD SERIES RINGS: 2
-*Entered the Hall of Fame in 1989*

Games	Caught Stealing %	Attempts	Thrown Out
2158	43.47	1078	468

YADIER MOLINA

NICKNAME: Yadi

HEIGHT: : 5 feet, 11 inches (180 cm)

WEIGHT: 220 lbs (99 kg)

YEARS ACTIVE: 2004–present*

TEAM: Cardinals

GOLD GLOVES: 6

ALL-STAR GAMES: 5

WORLD SERIES RINGS: 2

Games	Caught Stealing %	Attempts	Thrown Out
1,218	44.53	530	236

JOHNNY BENCH

The Cincinnati Reds' Johnny Bench is considered to be one of the greatest catchers in the game. He handled the pitching staff well and saved runs by blocking balls in the dirt. He also contributed with his bat, hitting 389 home runs and batting in 1,376 runs in 17 years. But it was his rifle of an arm behind the plate that many fans remember him for.

Bench caught more than 1,700 games in his big league career. During his career, he led the National League three times in runners caught stealing. He gunned down 469 would-be base stealers. His all-around stellar play led to two MVP awards, as well as the 1976 World Series MVP.

> "I can throw out any man alive."
>
> —*Johnny Bench*

> "I don't want to embarrass any other catcher by comparing him with Johnny Bench."
>
> —*Former Reds manager Sparky Anderson, when asked who compares to his catcher*

YADIER MOLINA

Yadier Molina is an elite catcher with a cannon for an arm. The Cardinals' backstop has thrown out nearly 45 percent of all base runners in his career, tops among active catchers. In 2005 he led the National League by throwing out an incredible 64 percent of runners.

Molina is known for his great instincts, guessing when players are going to steal. It keeps runners close to the base and takes pressure off of the pitcher. Teammate and pitcher Adam Wainwright talked about the value of pitching to Molina: "Guys get on base, you know you can bounce balls. You know you can throw balls to the corners, and he's going to make them look like strikes. He's going to throw guys out. He makes you believe in your stuff the way he talks to you on the mound."

"No offense to anybody else, but he's one in a million. He's so good."

—*Pitcher Jaime Garcia*

"Yadier Molina is the best catcher in baseball. He makes our job a lot easier."

—*Pitcher Adam Wainwright*

CLAYTON, KERSHAW

NICKNAME: The Claw
HEIGHT: 6 feet, 3 inches (190 cm)
WEIGHT: 220 lbs (99 kg)
YEARS ACTIVE: 2008–present*
TEAM: Dodgers
CY YOUNG AWARDS: 2
ALL-STAR GAMES: 3
-Led the NL in strikeouts twice

Games	Win-Loss Record	ERA	Strikeouts
84	77-46	2.60	1,206

*Stats are through the 2013 season.

NOLAN RYAN

NICKNAME: The Ryan Express
HEIGHT: 6 feet, 2 inches (188 cm)
WEIGHT: 170 lbs (77 kg)
YEARS ACTIVE: 1966, 1968–1993
TEAMS: Mets, Angels, Astros, Rangers
ALL-STAR GAMES: 8
WORLD SERIES RINGS: 1
-Led league in strikeouts 10 times
-Entered the Hall of Fame in 1999

Games	Win-Loss Record	ERA	Strikeouts
807	324-292	3.19	5,714

CLAYTON KERSHAW

Clayton "The Claw" Kershaw is the ace of the Los Angeles Dodgers pitching staff. Since the left-handed fireballer joined the Dodgers in 2008, the team has won its division three times. He collected his first Cy Young Award and won the pitching Triple Crown at age 23. During his 2011 Cy Young season, Kershaw tossed a complete-game shutout, defeating the Florida Marlins 8-0. He struck out 10 batters and had as many hits himself (two) as he gave up to the entire Marlins team.

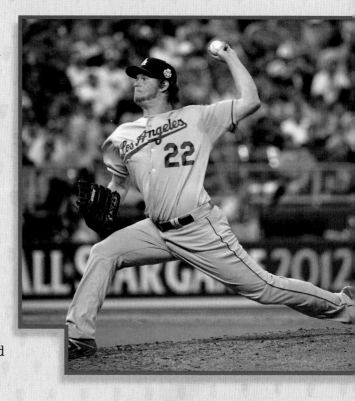

Kershaw struck out more than 1,100 batters by the time he turned 25. Many pitchers are just beginning their careers at that age. It is one reason players, coaches, and fans compare him to Dodgers legend Sandy Koufax.

"Kersh, at this point, is just different. The guys I've seen, it's hard to say anybody's better than that guy."

—*Dodgers manager and former player Don Mattingly*

"I have one goal that never changes, and that's to win every start." —*Clayton Kershaw*

Nolan Ryan built his Hall of Fame career over 27 seasons. With a fastball that regularly clocked over 100 mph, Ryan struck out a major league record 5,714 batters as a member of the New York Mets, California Angels, Houston Astros, and Texas Rangers. He ended his career with 324 wins.

The highlights of Ryan's career could fill an entire book on their own. But none was bigger than what the Ryan Express delivered on the evening of May 15, 1973. It was so cold only 12,000 fans were in the seats to watch Ryan master the Royals' lineup. He mowed down 27 batters without giving up a single hit. It was the first of a record seven no-hitters for Ryan, and it established him as one of the most dominant pitchers in his era.

"Ryan doesn't just get you out. He embarrasses you."
—*Former Oakland catcher Dave Duncan, on what it was like to hit against Ryan*

"It helps if the hitter thinks you're a little crazy." —*Nolan Ryan, explaining his success as a pitcher*

RANDY JO __ __

NICKNAME: The Big Unit
HEIGHT: 6 feet, 10 inches (208 cm)
WEIGHT: 225 lbs (102 kg)
YEARS ACTIVE: 1988–2009
TEAMS: Expos, Mariners, Astros, Diamondbacks, Yankees, Giants
CY YOUNG AWARDS: 5
ALL-STAR GAMES: 10
WORLD SERIES RINGS: 1
KNOWN FOR: Fastball

Games	Win-Loss Record	ERA	Strikeouts
682	303-166	3.29	4,875

SANDY KOUFAX

NICKNAME: The Left Arm of God
HEIGHT: 6 feet, 2 inches (188 cm)
WEIGHT: 210 lbs (95 kg)
YEARS ACTIVE: 1955–1966
TEAM: Dodgers
CY YOUNG AWARDS: 3
ALL-STAR GAMES: 7
MVP AWARDS: 1
WORLD SERIES RINGS: 4
KNOWN FOR: Curveball
-*Entered the Hall of Fame in 1972*

Games	Win-Loss Record	ERA	Strikeouts
397	165-87	2.76	2,396

TOM GLAVINE

NICKNAME: Tommy
HEIGHT: 6 feet (183 cm)
WEIGHT: 175 lbs (79 kg)
YEARS ACTIVE: 1987–2008
TEAMS: Braves, Mets
CY YOUNG AWARDS: 2
ALL-STAR GAMES: 10
WORLD SERIES RINGS: 1
KNOWN FOR: Changeup
-Entered the Hall of Fame in 2014

Games	Win-Loss Record	ERA	Strikeouts
682	305-203	3.54	2,607

IM WAKEFIELD

NICKNAME: Timmy Knuckles
HEIGHT: 6 feet, 2 inches (188 cm)
WEIGHT: 210 lbs (95 kg)
YEARS ACTIVE: 1992–1993, 1995–2011
TEAMS: Pirates, Red Sox
ALL-STAR GAMES: 1
WORLD SERIES RINGS: 2
KNOWN FOR: Knuckleball

Games	Win-Loss Record	ERA	Strikeouts
627	200-180	4.41	2,156

Five-time Cy Young Award winner Randy Johnson could reach 100 mph on the radar gun with ease. Johnson's fastball was especially harder to hit because of his height. His pitches came at hitters from a higher point than those of other pitchers. The Big Unit led the league in strikeouts nine times. During his 22-year career he averaged more than 10 strikeouts per nine innings pitched.

"It's like looking up at the top of a mountain."

—*Brian Giles, describing hitting against Johnson*

SANDY KOUFAX

Southpaw Sandy Koufax was a left-handed hitter's worst nightmare. Behind the strength of his curveball, Koufax led the

National League in strikeouts four times. He also recorded six consecutive 200-strikeout seasons. His 382 strikeouts in 1965 still stand as the most in a season by a left-handed pitcher. That year he earned the World Series MVP, going 2-1 with 29 strikeouts. After pitching a shutout in Game 5, Koufax came back on two days' rest to start Game 7. He blanked the Minnesota Twins again, securing a championship for the Dodgers.

"He's the best left-hander ever to play the game."

—*Pitcher Clayton Kershaw*

TOM GLAVINE

Tom Glavine made a living fooling hitters with his changeup. Glavine won 305 games behind his dominant changeup. During the 1995 World Series, Glavine put on a show with his off-speed magic. Glavine went 2-0 and only gave up four hits in two starts. He struck out 11 batters, and his Atlanta Braves defeated the Cleveland Indians to take home the championship.

"Tommy never gave in to any hitter. Ever."

—Former Braves pitching coach Leo Mazzone

TIM WAKEFIELD

Tim Wakefield's knuckleball was a headache for opposing hitters—and sometimes his own catcher. When his knuckleball

was "dancing," it was one of the toughest pitches to hit. Even the catcher wasn't sure where the pitch would end up. The unique pitch helped Wakefield earn 200 major league wins over his 19-year career.

"He's perfected a pitch that pretty much no one else throws." *—Infielder Dustin Pedroia*

MARIANO RIVERA

NICKNAME: The Sandman
HEIGHT: 6 feet, 2 inches (188 cm)
WEIGHT: 195 lbs (88 kg)
YEARS ACTIVE: 1995–2013
TEAM: Yankees
ALL-STAR GAMES: 13
WORLD SERIES RINGS: 5

-Led AL in saves three times
-All-time leader in saves

Games	Saves	ERA	Strikeouts	Win-Loss Record
1,115	652	2.21	1,173	82-60

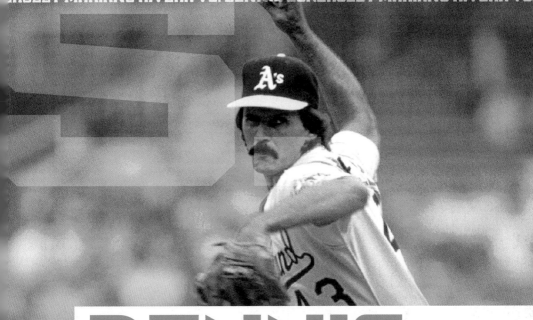

DENNIS
ECKERSLEY

NICKNAME: Eck
HEIGHT: 6 feet, 2 inches (188 cm)
WEIGHT: 190 lbs (86 kg)
YEARS ACTIVE: 1975–1998
TEAMS: Indians, Red Sox, Cubs, Athletics, Cardinals
ALL-STAR GAMES: 6
MVP AWARDS: 1
CY YOUNG AWARDS: 1
WORLD SERIES RINGS: 1
-Led AL in saves twice
-Entered the Hall of Fame in 2004

Games	Saves	ERA	Strikeouts	Win-Loss Record
1,071	390	3.50	2,401	197-171

MARIANO RIVERA

The bullpen door opened and Yankees closer Mariano Rivera jogged to the mound while "Enter Sandman" played on the loudspeaker. He had one job: Shut down the opponent and get the save. No man in the history of baseball has done it more times than Rivera. In 19 seasons, he appeared in more than 1,100 games and saved 652 of them. Teammates and fans came to expect that when the Yankees had the lead after eight innings, it was lights out.

Rivera shined the brightest when the pressure was on. In the 1999 World Series, he appeared in three of the four games, recording a win and two saves as the Yankees swept the Atlanta Braves. Rivera tossed 4⅔ shutout innings and was named MVP of the series. In 24 World Series games, Mo was 2-1 and recorded 11 saves with an ERA of 0.99.

"The other team knows that if they're losing in the eighth inning, they are going to lose."

—*Former closer Trevor Hoffman on Rivera's postseason pitching*

"Mo's broken a lot of my bats. He's broken a lot of everyone's bats. He keeps the bat companies in business." —*Outfielder Raul Ibanez*

DENNIS ECKERSLEY

> "You knew the hitter had no chance."
> —Former teammate Dave Henderson

> "My career spanned the era when relievers started to become more important."
> —Dennis Eckersley

Dennis Eckersley found success as both a starter and a closer. He spent the first half of his big league career as a starting pitcher. Eck tossed a no-hitter when he was with the Cleveland Indians in 1977. At the end of the season he was traded to the Red Sox and won 20 games in his first season in Boston. But it wasn't until Eckersley landed with the Oakland Athletics that his

career as a closer began. In 1988, in Eckersley's first season as a full-time closer, he led the league with 45 saves. But his most dominant season was in 1992 when he notched 51 saves for his team. The A's made the playoffs, and Eckersley won both the league MVP and the Cy Young Award, an honor rarely given to relievers.

Eck had a unique delivery style. He threw the ball sidearm to the plate. His pitching style helped make him a dominant closer. Hitters who spent eight innings facing a traditional over-the-top fastball struggled to adjust to the ball rising as it approached the plate.

MANAGER'S CALL

David Ortiz vs. Reggie Jackson

Mr. October had a knack for delivering the big hit in the postseason. But Red Sox fans know Big Papi delivers all season. Papi will drive in the winning run in April and still have plenty left to dominate pitchers in October. Ortiz is my clutch hitter.

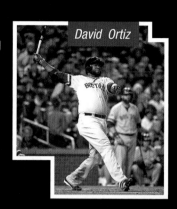
David Ortiz

Hank Aaron vs. Babe Ruth

Both men hit more than 700 home runs during their careers. Tough call, but I want the man many consider to be the true home run king of baseball. I'll take Hammerin' Hank on my team.

Rickey Henderson vs. Ty Cobb

The ability to steal bases can change the entire outcome of a game. Cobb played tough and stole plenty of bases, but Rickey is the all-time leader. In the bottom of the ninth, if I need an extra base to change the game, I want Rickey on my squad.

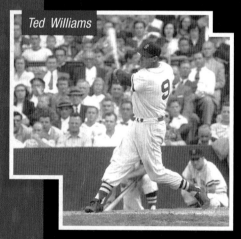
Ted Williams

Ted Williams vs. Miguel Cabrera

Ted Williams was the greatest hitter that ever lived and the last man to hit .400 in a single season. Miguel Cabrera won the Triple Crown in 2012 and has been a dominant hitter for a decade. I'd want them both, but in the end, I'll take The Splendid Splinter.

Derek Jeter vs. Ozzie Smith

The "Wizard of Oz" routinely made plays in the field that seemed impossible. But Jeter is as tough as they come and is a sure thing with his glove in the postseason. His defense anchored five World Series teams, so I'll go for the Yankees captain

Ken Griffey Jr. vs. Willie Mays

This was my toughest call to make. Both men were human highlight reels in the outfield. Griffey was known for robbing opposing hitters of home runs with incredible catches. But Mays will always be remembered for The Catch, so I'm going with The Say Hey Kid.

Johnny Bench vs. Yadier Molina

Molina is an elite catcher and has more good years ahead of him. But Bench had built a legacy with his cannon. I want Johnny behind the plate.

Nolan Ryan

Clayton Kershaw vs. Nolan Ryan

Many promising careers have been cut short by arm injuries. Kershaw's numbers are impressive, but he is still young. Ryan played for 27 years, struck out more than 5,700 batters, and tossed a record seven no-hitters. Kershaw is one of the best young arms in the game, but in my rotation, Ryan takes the spot.

Randy Johnson's fastball vs. Sandy Koufax's curveball vs. Tom Glavine's changeup vs. Tim Wakefield's knuckleball

I want them all on my team. But if I only get one, batters definitely feared the intimidating presence and blazing fastballs Johnson brought to the mound. The Big Unit narrowly makes the cut.

Mariano Rivera

Mariano Rivera vs. Dennis Eckersley

Eckersley won a Cy Young Award and tossed a no-hitter. But Rivera anchored five World Series championships for the Yankees and is the most dominant closer to ever play the game. No team is complete without Mo.

Critical Thinking Using the Common Core

1. What information on pages 6 and 7 supports the idea that David Ortiz and Reggie Jackson were clutch hitters? (Key Ideas and Details)

2. Read pages 32 through 39. Then list the pitchers in order based on how difficult you think it would be to hit against them. Support your answer with information found in the text. (Key Ideas and Details)

3. Look at the choices the author made on pages 44 and 45 in the Manager's Call section. Do you agree with the picks? Why or why not? Support your answer with information from this book as well as other books or online sources. (Integration of Knowledge and Ideas)

Quotation Sources

www.brainyquote.com, 6a, 11a, 14b, 19b, 43b; www.mlb.com, 6b, 11b, 26a, 34a, 43a; www.espn.go.com, 7a, 26b, 30b, 34b, 38a, 39a; www.usatoday.com, 7b; www.baberuth.com, 10a, 10b; www.nytimes.com, 14a, 39b; http://baseballguru.com, 15b; www.baseball-almanac.com, 15a, 18a, 18b, 22b, 30a, 35b; www.washingtonpost.com, 19a; www.jockbio.com, 22a; www.youtube.com, 23a, 31b; www.accessnorthga.com, 23b; www.theatlantic.com, 27a; www.baseballhall.org, 27b; www.news-leader.com, 31a; http://sabr.org, 35a; www.sportsonearth.com, 38b; www.nymag.com, 42a; http://msn.foxsports.com, 42b

Read More

Craats, Rennay. *Baseball.* New York: Weigl Publishers, 2010.

Doeden, Matt. *The World's Greatest Baseball Players.* North Mankato, Minn.: Capstone Press, 2010.

Rappoport, Ken. *Baseball's Top 10 Pitchers.* Berkeley Heights, N.J.: Enslow Publishers, 2010.

Rodriguez, Tania. *David Ortiz.* Broomall, Pa.: Mason Crest Publishers, 2012.

Internet Sites

FactHound offers a safe, fun way to find Internet sites related to this book. All of the sites on FactHound have been researched by our staff.

Here's all you do:

Visit *www.facthound.com*

Type in this code: 9781476561677

Super-cool stuff! Check out projects, games and lots more at **www.capstonekids.com**

Index

Aaron, Hank, 8, 10, 44
All-Star Games, 27
Atlanta Braves, 10, 39, 42

Barfield, Jesse, 26
Bench, Johnny, 28, 30, 45
Bonds, Barry, 10
Boston Red Sox, 6, 10, 18, 22, 27, 43, 44
Brock, Lou, 14

Cabrera, Miguel, 17, 19, 44
California Angels, 35
Cincinnati Reds, 30
Cleveland Indians, 27, 39, 43
Cobb, Ty, 13, 15, 44
Cy Young Awards, 34, 38, 43, 45

Detroit Tigers, 19

Eckersley, Dennis, 41, 43, 45

Florida Marlins, 34

Glavine, Tom, 37, 39, 45
Gold Gloves, 27
Griffey Jr., Ken, 24, 26, 45

Hall of Fame, 7, 11, 22, 30, 35
Henderson, Rickey, 12, 14, 44
Houston Astros, 35

Jackson, Reggie, 5, 7, 44
Jeter, Derek, 20, 22, 44
Johnson, Randy, 36, 38, 45

Kansas City Royals, 35
Kershaw, Clayton, 32, 34, 45
Koufax, Sandy, 34, 36, 38, 45

Los Angeles Dodgers, 7, 34, 38

Mays, Willie, 25, 27, 45
Milwaukee Brewers, 14
Minnesota Twins, 38
Molina, Yadier, 29, 31, 45
MVP awards, 30, 38, 42, 43

New York Giants, 27
New York Mets, 35
New York Yankees, 7, 22, 42, 44

Nixon, Trot, 22

Oakland Athletics, 14, 43
Ortiz, David, 4, 6, 44

Rivera, Mariano, 40, 42, 45
Ruth, Babe, 9, 11, 44
Ryan, Nolan, 33, 35, 45

Smith, Ozzie, 21, 23, 44
St. Louis Cardinals, 6, 31

Texas Rangers, 35
Triple Crown, 19, 34, 44

Wainwright, Adam, 31
Wakefield, Tim, 37, 39, 45
Wertz, Vic, 27
Williams, Ted, 16, 18, 44
World Series, 6, 7, 11, 27, 30, 38, 39, 42, 44, 45
World War II, 18

Yastrzemski, Carl, 19

Library of Congress Cataloging-in-Publication Data

Chandler, Matt.
  Side-by-side baseball stars : comparing pro baseball's greatest players / by Matt Chandler.
      pages cm.—(Sports Illustrated kids. Side-by-side sports)
  Includes bibliographical references and index.
  Summary: "Compares the greatest pro baseball players in history"—Provided by publisher.
  ISBN 978-1-4765-6167-7 (library binding)
  ISBN 978-1-4765-6172-1 (paperback)
  1. Baseball players—United States—Biography—Juvenile literature. 2. Baseball players—Rating of—Juvenile literature. I. Title.
  GV865.A1C394 2015
  796.3570922—dc23   2014007813

Editorial Credits

Anthony Wacholtz, editor; Ted Williams, designer; Eric Gohl, media researcher; Gene Bentdahl, production specialist

Photo Credits

Dreamstime: Jerry Coli, 35; Getty Images: Diamond Images/Kidwiler Collection, 25, NY Daily News Archive/Frank Hurley, 27; Library of Congress: 9, 11, 13, 15; Newscom: AFP/Jeff Kowalsky, 26, AFP/Mike Fiala, 14, Agence France Presse/Brian Bahr, 21, Ai Wire Photo Service/Chuck Rydlewski, 41, Everett Collection, 8, Icon SMI/Sporting News, 23, Icon SMI/TSN, 36 (bottom), 38 (bottom); Sports Illustrated: Bob Rosato, 37 (top), Damian Strohmeyer, 4, 6, 22, 37 (bottom), 39 (bottom), David E. Klutho, 19, 29, 31, 34, 44 (top), Heinz Kluetmeier, 12, 43, Hy Peskin, 44 (bottom), John Biever, 17, 42, John G. Zimmerman, cover (bottom), 16, 18, John Iacono, 5, 7, 33, 36 (top), 39 (top), John W. McDonough, 32, Manny Millan, 45 (top), Robert Beck, cover (top), 20, 38 (top), 45 (bottom), Simon Bruty, 40, Tony Triolo, 10, V.J. Lovero, 24, Walter Iooss Jr., 28, 30

Design Elements: Shutterstock